The
Beaded Jewelry
for A
Wedding
Book

# INTERSTELLAR

## TRADING & PUBLISHING COMPANY

LA MESA, CALIFORNIA

**ISBN** 0-9645957-5-3
**LIBRARY OF CONGRESS CATALOG NUMBER: 96-94611**
**SAN: 298-5829**

All illustrations by Wendy Simpson Conner
Color Photography by Don Brandos
Printed in the United States of America

FIRST PRINTING: JULY, 1997

ACKNOWLEDGMENTS:
*To Jennie, Priscilla, Joni and Paul;*
*and everyone who bought and loved*
*THE BEST LITTLE BEADING BOOK,*
*THE BEADED LAMPSHADE BOOK,*
*THE MAGICAL BEADED MEDICINE BAG BOOK.*
*THE 'KNOTTY' MACRAME AND BEADING BOOK*
*THE BEADED WATCHBAND  BOOK*
*&*
*THE CHAIN & CRYSTAL  BOOK*

# Introduction

There are times when it seems that everyone you know is getting married! One summer, I attended eight weddings. After the third or fourth, they all sort of "morphed" together. Each bride seemed to be wearing almost the same pair of earrings. Even the bridesmaids seemed to be wearing the same necklace. This intrigued me, so I visited a bridal shop. There were three large rooms of gowns, dresses, shoes, etc., but only one little woebegone jewelry display on the counter. When I asked the salesperson why there was so little choice, she told me that most brides don't care about jewelry (yeah, right). She also said that most cared more about their headpiece.

A trip to the "headpiece" department confirmed why there was such an emphasis placed on headpieces: a few beads and silk flowers mounted on a wire frame with florist's tape sold for $170.00! Having worked with beads and related supplies my whole life, I looked at these headpieces and realized that there was maybe $15.00 in materials in each one. The most expensive one was $220.00. When I asked why this was so much more than the others, the salesperson told me "because the beads are pink". Hmmm. Well, wheels started turning, and this book was born.

Weddings cost so much nowadays, that the jewelry a bride and the wedding party wears should be elegant and appropriate, but not ridiculously priced. Many brides settle for something they really don't like because they can't find anything better. Usually, the bride's mom or aunt, or even the bride herself has done beadwork. Making the wedding jewelry never occurs to a lot of people.

The benefit of making your own is that you will always have exactly what your want. You can coordinate each member of the wedding party's jewelry, so that bridesmaids, flowergirls, mothers of both bride and groom, all work together. You can make your own gifts to give your bridesmaids, or even little thank you gifts for the people who helped in special little ways. You can even have a beading party with your friends - each bridemaid makes her own necklace.This is a great way to cut the cost of the wedding: you can always make things for less than it costs to buy them readymade! There are a lot of different designs in this book . . . from the traditional to the more contemporary. They are all easy to make, and there's even a couple of headpieces. Have fun!

This is part of a series of 25 books called **The Beading Books Series.** Other books in the series include *The Best Little Beading Book, The Beaded Lampshade Book, The Magical Beaded Medicine Bag Book, The "Knotty" Macrame and Beading Book, The Beaded Watchband Book* and *The Chain & Crystal Book.*

As always, I love hearing your wonderful comments. Please feel free to write to me c/o The Interstellar Trading and Publishing Company, Post Office Box 2215, La Mesa, CA 91943.

**Happy Beading!™**

"Me"

# Table of Contents

# Beads and Materials

These projects are actually a lot easier than they look. The secret to making them is in the selection of materials and tools. You don't have to spend a lot; just be aware of quality differences when you buy them.

## *Pearls*

There are so many types of beads to choose from. Of course, pearls are the most traditional for weddings.

There are different types of pearls. The acrylic ones are very inexpensive. Some look very nice, but others look cheap. Always use the nicer ones (sometimes it's worth spending a little more for a better quality). Because these are your least expensive, they can be used in places where you'll need a lot. You can embellish your gown with these, but be VERY careful if you take it to the dry cleaners. Some of the chemicals they use will melt these acrylics. If you are using these beads on clothing, I recommend taking the beads into the cleaners for them to assess before you even start beading, or even make a little test swatch to see if they can withstand the harsh chemicals.

Glass pearls also work for clothing. They look a lot like real pearls, but some tend to scratch. Again, choose with the dry cleaners in mind.

For jewelry making, fresh water pearls offer a beautiful alternative. They are a fraction of the price of saltwater pearls (i.e., cultured), yet some of them look just like the more expensive ones. They come in a variety of shapes. The coating on a pearl is called "nacre", and it is actually very fragile, and can scratch. You'll find the best prices for these at gem show s or bead stores. "Pearl boutiques" will charge too much. Look for pearls with deep color and lustre. They come in white, offwhite, or a variety of colors. Some colors are natural, some are enhanced. It is not recommended to use these on clothing, as real pearls tend to dissolve if left in water or chemicals for a long time.

Other types of pearls include cultured pearls (usually very expensive), "popcorn pearls" (a type of freshwater pearl, they're elegant yet inexpensive), "champaigne pearls" (beautiful mauve freshwater pearl), "gunmetal pearls" (rich, pewtertone freshwater pearl), and "seed pearls" (very small freshwater pearl).

To care for pearls, simply wipe with a damp cloth. Store necklaces and earrings in a jewelry box away from dampness. Be careful if you spray hairspray or perfume near pearls . . . it dulls the finish.

## Other Beads

Crystal beads are also used for wedding jewelry. I like the Czech crystal the most, because it isn't as brittle as the Austrian, and is a lot less expensive. They come in beautiful colors with a lot of radiance.

Semiprecious beads are so beautiful to add - garnet, rose quartz, blue topaz, rainbow moonstone, amethyst . . . even turquoise! You can coordinate your stones to your wedding colors.

Also think about using glass beads . . . Czech lampwork beads are so lovely and romantic looking - they add so much to any design.

## Findings

A finding is anything that is not a bead. For example, clasps, metal enhancers, pendants, etc. One of my goals with this book was to use unusual adornments, but still keep the "wedding look". I've used pendants with semiprecious stones to tie a look together. Many of these can be obtained at gem shows and bead stores, or through mail order catalogues.

Many people like gold findings, but sterling silver is also very popular. Look for unusual sterling beads that compliment your other findings.

To create special effects, use separator bars and elegant clasps (please see the *Multistrand Bride's Choker*). The illustrations below show other findings.

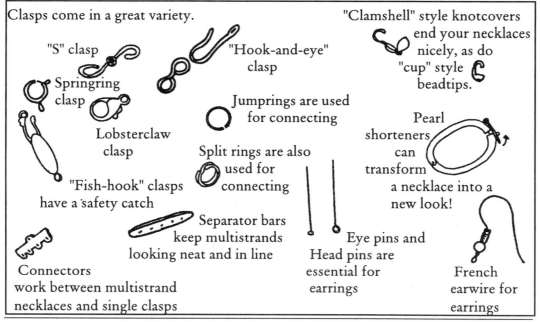

Clasps come in a great variety.

"S" clasp

"Hook-and-eye" clasp

"Clamshell" style knotcovers end your necklaces nicely, as do "cup" style beadtips.

Springring clasp

Lobsterclaw clasp

Jumprings are used for connecting

Split rings are also used for connecting

Pearl shorteners can transform a necklace into a new look!

"Fish-hook" clasps have a safety catch

Separator bars keep multistrands looking neat and in line

Eye pins and Head pins are essential for earrings

French earwire for earrings

Connectors work between multistrand necklaces and single clasps

# Tools and Other Supplies

You really won't need to purchase a lot of tools to make these projects. Depending on the projects you choose, you should only need a few things.

## Needles

The most useful is a little twisted wire needle that works great with pearls and other beads. It has a collapsible eye and is very 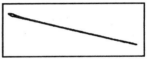 flexible. It fits through most beads (including pearls) easily. However, it's not super-sturdy, and won't last through many necklaces.

The number 10 or 12 English beading needle works best when embellishing fabric with beads. It is very slender and thin, and works well with seedbeads or any smaller bead.

## Threads

The most used thread is a silk or nylon bead cord. You can purchase this on a card with a needle already attached, or by the spool. It comes in different weights. "F" (#3) is your general purpose weight that works with most beads. For pearls, you may want to use "B" (#2) weight. Always calibrate the size of your thread to the size of the hole in the bead. This becomes even more important when you are knotting between the beads. Too thin a thread will produce knots that the bead just slides over; if it's too thick, you won't be able to get the beads on the thread.

For embellishing fabric or making the headpieces, nymo works well. This is a thin nylon that comes on a little bobbin. It's like a regular sewing thread, but stronger. Nymo lasts for years, and is perfect for working with smaller beads. I do not recommend using it on larger beads . . . it's too thin. This also comes in weights, but they don't correspond to the other cords.

## Tools
Pointed tweezers are necessary for knotwork.

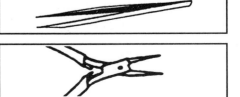

Chain nose pliers are useful for making earrings.

---

When designing your necklaces, it's always a good idea to take into account the style of dress that will be worn. Size of beads, length of necklace, and colors that work together are all governed by the dresses worn. You don't want your necklace and neckline to clash. Here are nine of the most common necklines.

The shortest necklaces are called Chokers (or Collars). They are worn at the throat, usually about 15" long (depending on the individual's necksize).

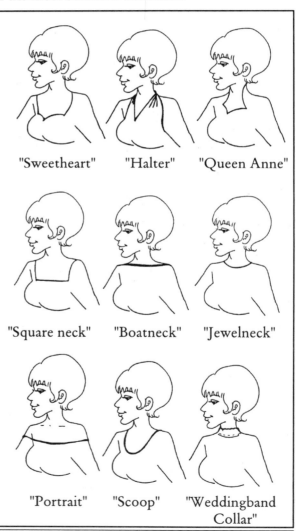

"Sweetheart"  "Halter"  "Queen Anne"

"Square neck"  "Boatneck"  "Jewelneck"

"Portrait"  "Scoop"  "Weddingband Collar"

The Princess length is about 18" long.

The Matinee is 20 to 24 inches long.

The Opera is 28 to 30 inches.

The Lariat or Rope is 45 inches or longer.

The only rules that govern what you should and shouldn't wear are common sense: you don't want your necklace to get lost in the neckline of your dress; you don't want it to tangle or conflict with the design. Otherwise, anything goes!

# *Pearl Knotting*

The mark of a fine pearl necklace is usually determined by whether or not there are knots between each pearl. While not an absolute necessity, knotting does protect the pearls from rubbing and scratching each other. A necklace that has been knotted always has an expensive look to it; even inexpensive beads take on a more stylish glow.

It does take a little practice to make this perfect, but once you get the rhythm, there will be no stopping you! I suggest you practice on very inexpensive beads, and work up to the more elaborate beads and designs. This way you won't get frustrated.

You'll first want to choose your thread. As mentioned before, calibrate the thickness of the thread to the size of the hole in the bead. Take the beads with you when you buy your thread, so you know it will match.

When you're first starting out, you're better off buying the silk thread that comes on those little cards. There are approximately 6 meters per card (over 6 yards), and the thread is already doubled with a needle attached. This saves you having to figure length and thread the needle. You can easily get one necklace out of this card, sometimes two (depending on the size thread and length of finished necklace).

If you have many, many necklaces to make, than you're better off buying a little spool of silk (it's more economical) plus several of the twisted wire needles.

## Measuring Your Thread

In knotting, a good safe way to measure your thread is to figure that you should cut off 5 times the length you wish to end up with. So, if you want a 20" necklace, cut 100 inches of thread from your spool. Thread your needle, then tie your two ends together (you always work double thread - this will last much longer and be a stronger necklace). You now have 50 inches of thread. Why do you do this? Because when you knot, each knot eats up a little thread. By the time you get done, you may have 100 knots. That is several inches just in knots!

## Materials You'll Need

For a single strand, you will need thread, a needle, and beads, but you'll also need a clasp and 2 knot covers (just for the ends). You can use either the Clamshell style (which hides your knots) or the Cup style (which is considered traditional with pearls). You'll also need a pair of very pointy tweezers, and cement for securing your beginning and ending knots.

---

## Getting Started

After measuring, cut the right length of thread. Thread your needle, and double the thread so that when you make your knot, both tails are together. Make an overhand knot about 2 inches from the end away from the needle. Add a knot

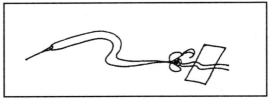

cover. Be careful that you put in on in the right direction: the hook should face out (this will connect to your clasp). Using scotch tape, secure this to the table in front of you (I tape to the right; you may find that taping to the left is easier)

Next, make an overhand knot just after your knot cover. This stabilizes the end. Use your tweezers. YOU MUST PUT THE TIP OF THE TWEEZER INTO THE LOOP OF THE OVERHAND KNOT FOR THIS TO WORK! The tweezer guides the knot down to the tip.

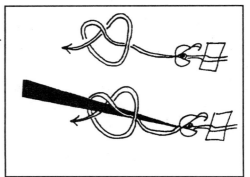

As you pull the end with the needle to tighten the knot, be aware of the way that the thread should be traveling down the shaft of the tweezers, which should be lightly gripping the place where you want the knot to be.THE KNOT WILL END UP WHEREVER THE TIP OF THE TWEEZERS IS.

When you have pulled all the way, stop pulling the thread as you CAREFULLY pull out the tweezers. Then, take your two strands, and lift and separate them to pull the knot back against the knot cover, as closely as possible.

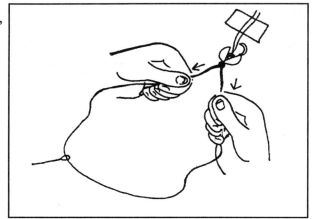

Add a bead, and repeat the same knotting process. Keep repeating until you have the desired length. Add tape as needed to hold your work steady. You'll work a lot faster if your beads don't flop around.

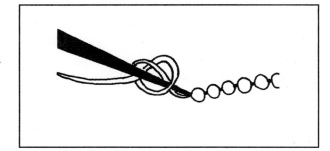

When you get to the end, add your second knot cover (remember, it should be in the opposite direction to the first one. They should both have that hook facing out).

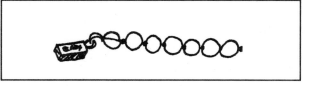

Cement the knots at the ends only (the ones in the knot covers). If you've used a clamshell style knotcover, close it after you've cemented. Trim your end threads. Attach to your clasp.

# Color Photo Index

Mr. & Mrs. J. Lombards
request the honor of your presence
at
the wedding
of
their daughter,
Crystal Pearl
to
Jasper Obsidian
on
Wednesday, February 14, 2000

# *Making a Simple Earring*

Using a plier to make your own earrings is a great way to save money, and yet still have exactly what you want. You can also use this technique for making dangles and drops on your bracelets or necklaces.

You'll want two of everything (for two earrings). You'll need head or eye pins, two of every bead, and earwires.

First, thread your beads on a pin in the desired order.

Cut the pin with wirecutters 1/2 inch from the top of the bead.

Bend the top of the post at an angle with your pliers

Thread the earwire on post.

With your pliers, bend the post to make a nice, smooth loop.

Finish by making sure that the loop is closed nice and tight.

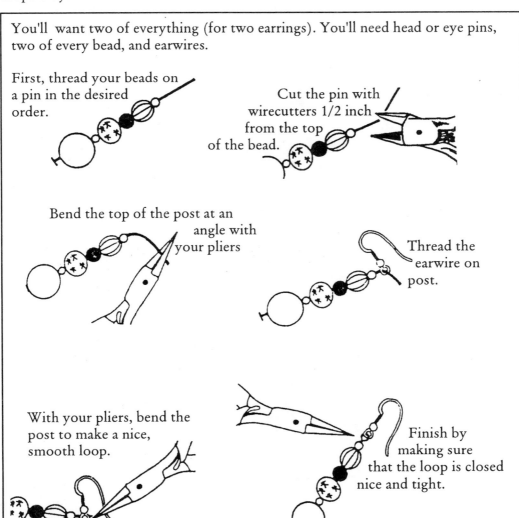

# Earring Designs

First comes the dress, then the emphasis is on jewelry. Generally, brides wear fairly simple earrings so they don't detract from the rest of the outfit, or get caught in the headpiece. Here are some simple earring designs. For more elaborate designs, please see *The Best Little Beading Book,* which I also wrote. There are many more involved designs there.

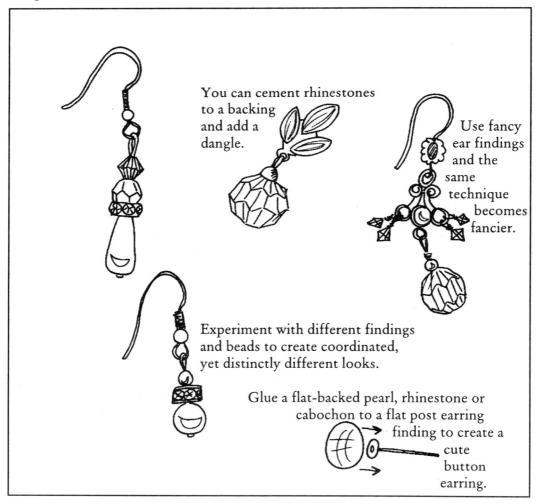

You can cement rhinestones to a backing and add a dangle.

Use fancy ear findings and the same technique becomes fancier.

Experiment with different findings and beads to create coordinated, yet distinctly different looks.

Glue a flat-backed pearl, rhinestone or cabochon to a flat post earring finding to create a cute button earring.

One of the easiest ways to make jewelry is to use memory wire. This is a coil of wire that retains its shape. It's fast and easy for bracelets and necklaces.

Bracelets are usually done in a coil (one long length is cut off and wrapped around the wrist several times). Necklaces are usually single strand, or several strands joined by separator bars. It's not a good idea to wrap the wire around your neck - it could get too tight!

To work with memory wire, you'll need a chain nose plier and a wire cutter. Most beads will thread on easily. The nice thing is, because you're using a wire, you won't need a needle!

## *To make a simple coiled bracelet:*

**MATERIALS NEEDED:**
- A length of memory wire five coils long
- Enough beads to fill (appx. 16") wire
- One head pin (optional)
- Your pliers

By the time you add your beads, this bracelet will only be about 3 coils long.

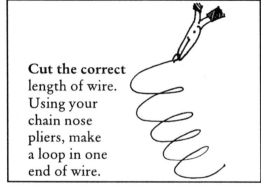

**Cut the correct** length of wire. Using your chain nose pliers, make a loop in one end of wire.

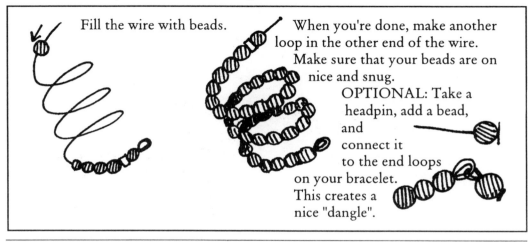

Fill the wire with beads.

When you're done, make another loop in the other end of the wire. Make sure that your beads are on nice and snug.

OPTIONAL: Take a headpin, add a bead, and connect it to the end loops on your bracelet. This creates a nice "dangle".

It's very easy to make a single strand memory wire choker.

## MATERIALS NEEDED:
- A length of memory wire long enough to go around the neck once
- Thirty-six 7x5mm aqua crystal
- Twenty-eight 3mm crystal rondells
- Ten rhinestone rondells
- One pendant (optional)
- Your pliers and wire cutters

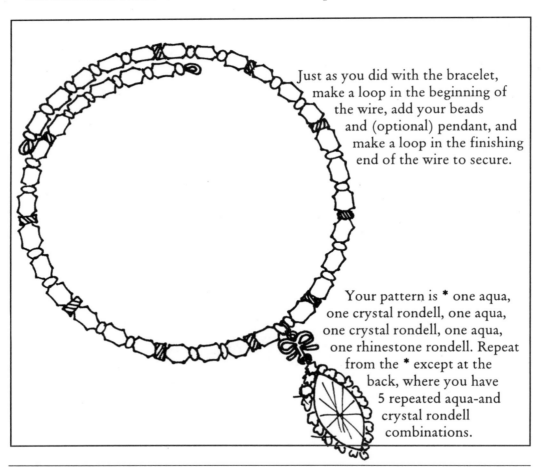

Just as you did with the bracelet, make a loop in the beginning of the wire, add your beads and (optional) pendant, and make a loop in the finishing end of the wire to secure.

Your pattern is * one aqua, one crystal rondell, one aqua, one crystal rondell, one aqua, one rhinestone rondell. Repeat from the * except at the back, where you have 5 repeated aqua-and crystal rondell combinations.

It's a little more involved when you want to work with multiple strands, but it makes a very elegant choker.

## MATERIALS NEEDED:
- Three lengths of memory wire , each one long enough to go around the neck once
- Sixty 6mm pearls
- Size 8 seedbeads (get extra so you can adjust your pattern if necessary)
- One three-channel center      - One head pin (optional)
- Six separator bars      - Your pliers and wire cutters

The secret to making this elegant choker is in using separator bars to keep the 3 strands in place. In this particular necklace, the two outer strands are the same, with the center one a different pattern of beads. The outer patterns are alternating 6mm pearls with size 8 irridescent seedbeads. Six separator bars (and the center, which has channels for three strands) holds this in place. The center strand is just the seedbeads. This creates a nice sense of balance.

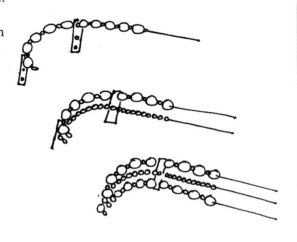

You'll cut the 3 pieces of wire, then add your loop to the starting end of the first strand. Add your beads in your pattern. Place your separator bars at interval. You can work all three strands at the same time if you like, or you can finish one and then go on to the next.

You can add an optional dangle if you like.

# Chain and Pearl Necklaces

These elegant necklaces are popular for all occasions. Here are two variations. The only differences are the chains and pearls used.

## MATERIALS NEEDED:
- One sixteen inch chain, either sterling or gold filled
- Seven coordinating head pins (gold with gold, silver with silver)
- Seven pearls                              - Seven 2 or 3mm gold or silver beads
- Your pliers

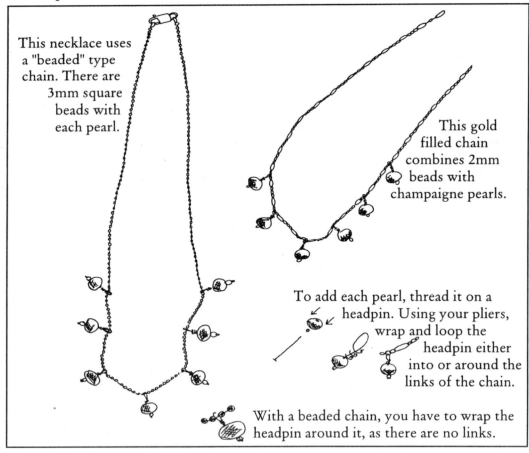

This necklace uses a "beaded" type chain. There are 3mm square beads with each pearl.

This gold filled chain combines 2mm beads with champaigne pearls.

To add each pearl, thread it on a headpin. Using your pliers, wrap and loop the headpin either into or around the links of the chain.

With a beaded chain, you have to wrap the headpin around it, as there are no links.

# *Modified Chain Necklace*

This is a great way to show off a beautiful pendant. As long as your chain will fit through the pendant, there is no limit as to what you can do!

## MATERIALS NEEDED:
- A length of chain
- Four 6mm pearls, eight amethyst rondells, and eight amber rondells
- A pendant that coordinates these stones (or any of your choice)
- Four eye pins or 24 gauge wire          - Your pliers and wire cutters

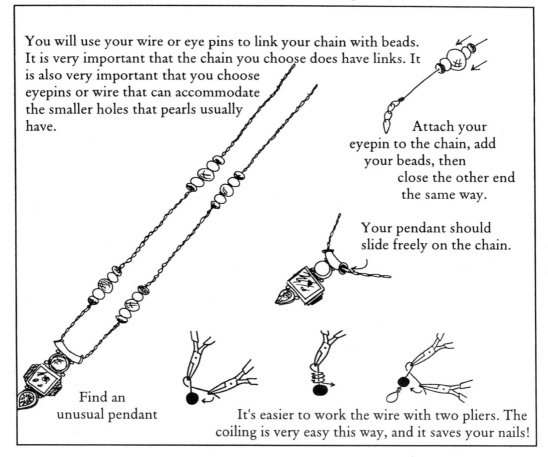

You will use your wire or eye pins to link your chain with beads. It is very important that the chain you choose does have links. It is also very important that you choose eyepins or wire that can accommodate the smaller holes that pearls usually have.

Attach your eyepin to the chain, add your beads, then close the other end the same way.

Your pendant should slide freely on the chain.

Find an unusual pendant

It's easier to work the wire with two pliers. The coiling is very easy this way, and it saves your nails!

This necklace has popped up in all the latest movies and television shows. It's easy to make, and takes very few materials. Your bare thread will show, which makes it fun to use colors. Use the silk thread that comes on the cards - it has a little crease that makes it easier to measure out the spacing between beads.

**MATERIALS NEEDED:**
- One card of silk thread in a size appropriate for knotting with your beads
- Lamp beads or pearls
- Two knot covers and a clasp
- Cement
- Your tweezers

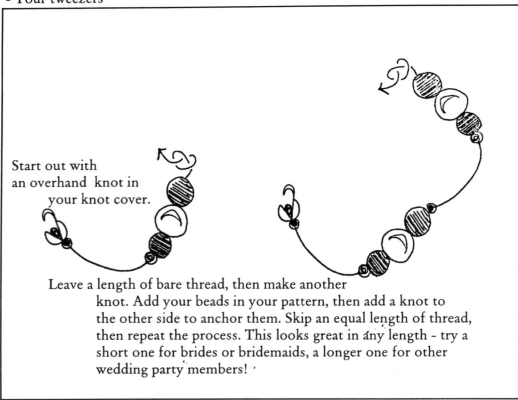

Start out with
an overhand knot in
    your knot cover.

Leave a length of bare thread, then make another
    knot. Add your beads in your pattern, then add a knot to
    the other side to anchor them. Skip an equal length of thread,
    then repeat the process. This looks great in any length - try a
    short one for brides or bridemaids, a longer one for other
    wedding party members!

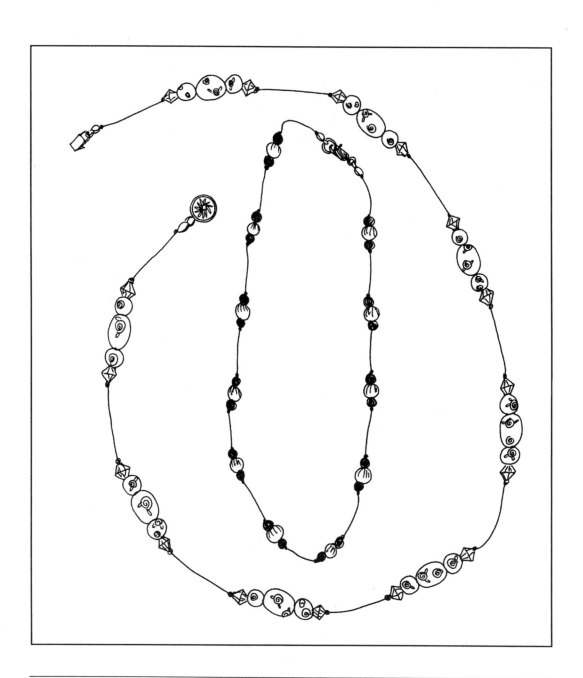

Stringing a necklace without knotting between beads is a piece of cake! Again, calibrate the thread to the size of the holes in the beads. Use your knot covers for your ends. This goes a lot faster than knotting!

Thread your needle, and make an overhand knot using both tails of the thread.

Add the first knot cover, with the needle going from the inside to outside. If done properly, the cup part of the knot cover is covering the knot. The loop is facing out. Add your beads, then the second knot cover, in the opposite direction than the first.

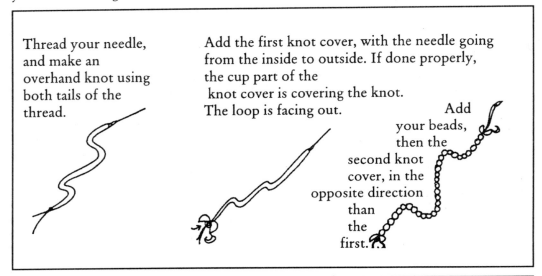

Make a couple of square knots tightly in the clamshell of the knot cover (or in the cup of the cup style).

if the thread keeps wanting to slip out.

# Garnet and Silver Necklace

Using the basic stringing techniques shown, you can make anything! This garnet necklace works up very quickly.

MATERIALS NEEDED:
- One 16" strand of 4mm garnets
- Sixteen 2mm sterling beads
- One sterling clasp and two sterling knot covers
- One pendant (I've used a sterling cross with a garnet)
- Silk thread and a twisted wire needle
- Cement

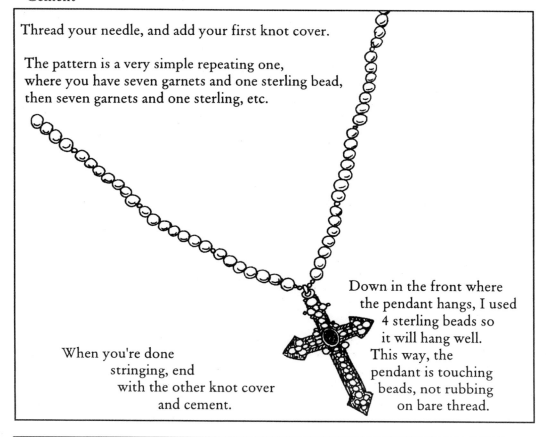

Thread your needle, and add your first knot cover.

The pattern is a very simple repeating one, where you have seven garnets and one sterling bead, then seven garnets and one sterling, etc.

When you're done stringing, end with the other knot cover and cement.

Down in the front where the pendant hangs, I used 4 sterling beads so it will hang well. This way, the pendant is touching beads, not rubbing on bare thread.

Irridescent seedbeads and marbelized glass combine to make one elegant necklace! You can make this one longer to work with more tailored necklines.

## MATERIALS NEEDED:
- Irridescent size 10 or 11 seedbeads
- Five 10mm bronze marbelized glass beads
- Ten 8mm mauve marbelized glass beads
- Ten 10x14mm teardrop shaped crystal
- One gold clasp and two knot covers
- Silk thread in "B" weight and one twisted wire needle
- Cement

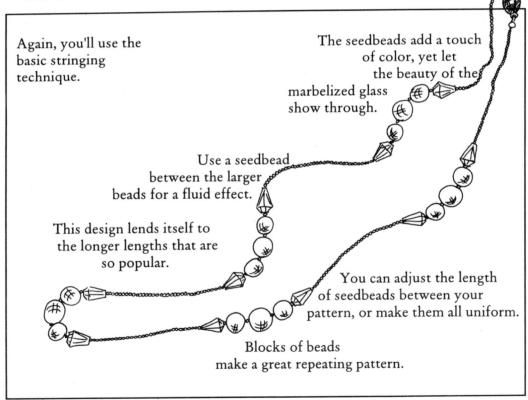

Again, you'll use the basic stringing technique.

The seedbeads add a touch of color, yet let the beauty of the marbelized glass show through.

Use a seedbead between the larger beads for a fluid effect.

This design lends itself to the longer lengths that are so popular.

You can adjust the length of seedbeads between your pattern, or make them all uniform.

Blocks of beads make a great repeating pattern.

# *Moonstone and Pearl Necklace*

Moonstone is a very beautiful stone, and Rainbow Moonstone (sometimes called Blue Moonstone) is even more lovely. It glows with a radiance like an Opal. This necklace combines this beautiful stone with Peridot and pearls, and the result in quite elegant. Even without the enhancer (which is removable), this is a dazzler!

MATERIALS NEEDED:
- Thirty-six moonstone rondells
- Sixteen 5mm round moonstone beads
- Thirty-six peridot rondells
- Eighteen 6x8mm freshwater "potato" pearls
- One clasp and two knot covers
- Silk thread and one twisted wire needle
- Enhancer (optional)
- Cement

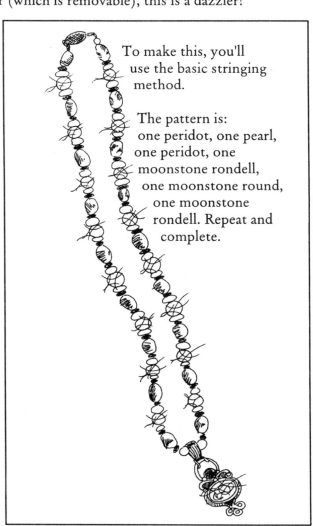

To make this, you'll use the basic stringing method.

The pattern is: one peridot, one pearl, one peridot, one moonstone rondell, one moonstone round, one moonstone rondell. Repeat and complete.

This is the necklace shown on the cover. You can see how the Moonstone just glows! This is a wonderful stone for a bride to wear - Moonstone is considered the most feminine of stones. It is considered a very lucky stone for women.

Many women used to wear it when they were in labor because it was said to ease the pain.

# Turquoise and Pearl Necklace

Turquoise is usually not associated with wedding jewelry, and that's what makes this necklace all the more special. By teaming turquoise, garnets, pearls and sterling, you have a unique necklace that people respond to so positively!

**MATERIALS NEEDED:**
- Eighty-eight 6mm pearls
- Six 6mm turquoise beads
- Twenty seven 2mm garnets
- Twelve 5mm sterling silver beads
- Clasp and 2 knot covers
- Silk thread and needle
- Turquoise pendant (optional)
- Cement

Using the basic stringing technique, you'll work this necklace in the following pattern: 13 pearls, *one garnet, one silver bead, one garnet, one turquoise, one garnet, one silver, one garnet, 7 pearls, (repeat from the * until you have 3 sets of 7 pearls. Ending with that set, Use 3garnets down in the center so your pendant is resting on them. This helps to protect your thread. Continue back up the other side with the same pattern.

# *Pearl and Sterling Necklace*

This looks fabulous with a "boat" or "weddingband" neckline. You can use a cherished locket, or an antique pocketwatch, or any unusual larger center for this.

MATERIALS NEEDED:
- Ninety-three 5mm pearls
- Six 10mm sterling ornamental beads
- Eighty sterling spacer disks (or rondells)
- Twelve 2mm sterling beads (optional)
- One pendant (locket, enhancer, pocketwatch, etc.)
- Clasp and 2 knot covers
- Silk thread and needle

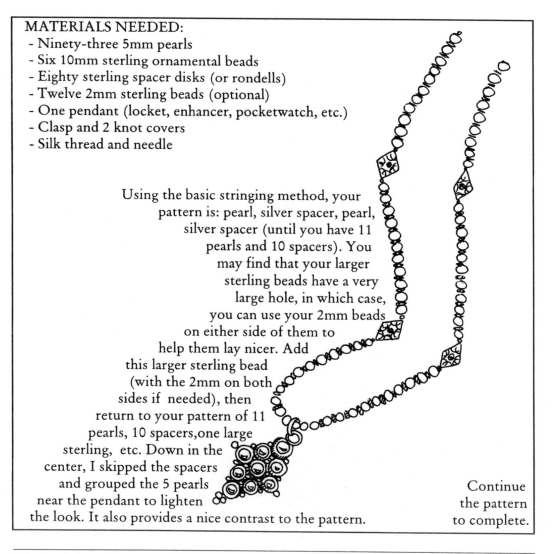

Using the basic stringing method, your pattern is: pearl, silver spacer, pearl, silver spacer (until you have 11 pearls and 10 spacers). You may find that your larger sterling beads have a very large hole, in which case, you can use your 2mm beads on either side of them to help them lay nicer. Add this larger sterling bead (with the 2mm on both sides if needed), then return to your pattern of 11 pearls, 10 spacers, one large sterling, etc. Down in the center, I skipped the spacers and grouped the 5 pearls near the pendant to lighten the look. It also provides a nice contrast to the pattern.

Continue the pattern to complete.

# Amethyst and Amber Necklace

The rich jeweltones of this piece look almost gothic. Amber and amethyst are a beautiful combination, and with the pearls, it is a stunning piece. Make this for the bride, bridesmaids, or even as a shower gift!

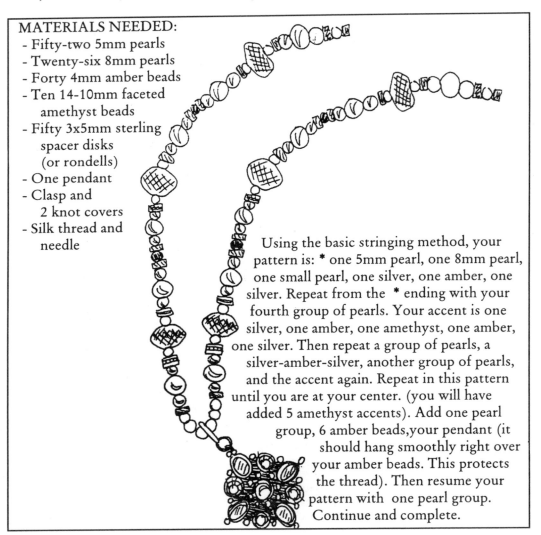

**MATERIALS NEEDED:**
- Fifty-two 5mm pearls
- Twenty-six 8mm pearls
- Forty 4mm amber beads
- Ten 14-10mm faceted amethyst beads
- Fifty 3x5mm sterling spacer disks (or rondells)
- One pendant
- Clasp and 2 knot covers
- Silk thread and needle

Using the basic stringing method, your pattern is: * one 5mm pearl, one 8mm pearl, one small pearl, one silver, one amber, one silver. Repeat from the * ending with your fourth group of pearls. Your accent is one silver, one amber, one amethyst, one amber, one silver. Then repeat a group of pearls, a silver-amber-silver, another group of pearls, and the accent again. Repeat in this pattern until you are at your center. (you will have added 5 amethyst accents). Add one pearl group, 6 amber beads, your pendant (it should hang smoothly right over your amber beads. This protects the thread). Then resume your pattern with one pearl group. Continue and complete.

This makes a nice set to wear at the wedding, or give as a gift to the bridesmaids. To give this set a little extra, the beads have been knotted between. A rich purple thread was used, so that the color of the knots matches the beads.

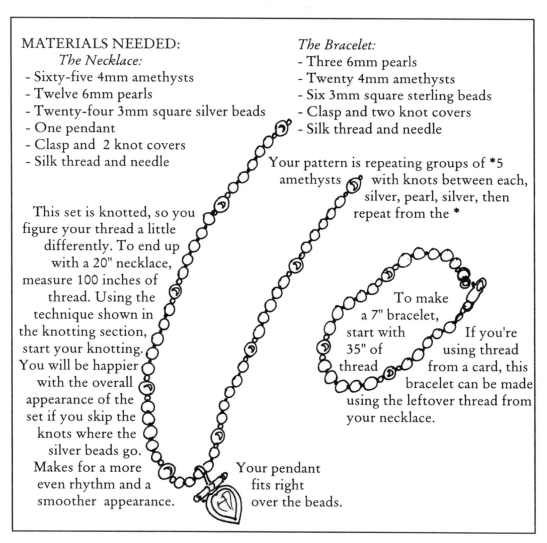

MATERIALS NEEDED:

*The Necklace:*
- Sixty-five 4mm amethysts
- Twelve 6mm pearls
- Twenty-four 3mm square silver beads
- One pendant
- Clasp and 2 knot covers
- Silk thread and needle

*The Bracelet:*
- Three 6mm pearls
- Twenty 4mm amethysts
- Six 3mm square sterling beads
- Clasp and two knot covers
- Silk thread and needle

Your pattern is repeating groups of *5 amethysts with knots between each, silver, pearl, silver, then repeat from the *

This set is knotted, so you figure your thread a little differently. To end up with a 20" necklace, measure 100 inches of thread. Using the technique shown in the knotting section, start your knotting. You will be happier with the overall appearance of the set if you skip the knots where the silver beads go. Makes for a more even rhythm and a smoother appearance.

To make a 7" bracelet, start with 35" of thread. If you're using thread from a card, this bracelet can be made using the leftover thread from your necklace.

Your pendant fits right over the beads.

Popcorn pearls are as delicious to look at as they sound! They are nubby, bumpy freshwater pearls that range in color from champaigne to soft beige to white. They are so elegant! This simple necklace works up very quickly, and is sure to get compliments.

MATERIALS NEEDED:
   - Two sixteen inch strands of popcorn pearls (to make a 32" necklace)
   - Two knot covers and a clasp
   - Silk thread and needle

This is done in the basic stringing method. This is a nice, easy one to make . . . there's no pattern! simply string your pearls as they come off the temporary strands - any order will do.

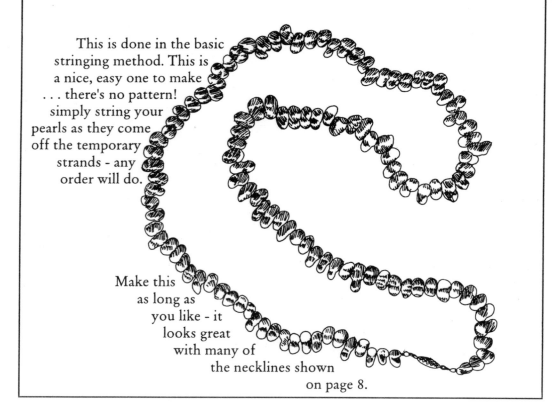

Make this as long as you like - it looks great with many of the necklines shown on page 8.

The classic bride's necklace is a string of graduated sized pearls. I think eveyone's mom was married in such a necklace (mine was). This has that Grace Kelly sort of elegance that looks dashing with almost any neckline.

MATERIALS NEEDED:
- Sixty 3mm pearls
- Ten 4mm pearls
- Six 4 1/2mm pealrs
- Eight 5mm pearls
- Six 6mm pearls
- Eight 7mm pearls
- Two 8 1/2mm pealrs
- Two 9mm pearls
- One 10mm pearl
- Two knot covers and a clasp
- Silk thread and needle

Lay your pearls out according to size. The larger ones go in the front. You can pearlknot, or it looks equally elegant without knots.

The enhancers make this pearl necklace look like a million dollars.

**MATERIALS NEEDED:**
- Fifty-eight 5mm pearls
- Nine pearl enhancers
- One clasp and two knot covers
- Silk thread and needle

Using the basic stringing method, add 17 pearls, then one enhancer, 3 pearls, one enhancer, etc. Use all of your enhancers. Finish with the remaining pearls.

String the enhancers right along with the pearls.

# Flower Girl's Necklace

This sweet necklace works for everyone, not just the flower girls.

MATERIALS NEEDED:
- Twenty-four 10x4mm rose quartz beads
- Twenty-six 4mm opalescent glass beads
- Forty-eight 2mm gold spacer beads
- One heart pendant
- One clasp and two knot covers
- Silk thread and needle

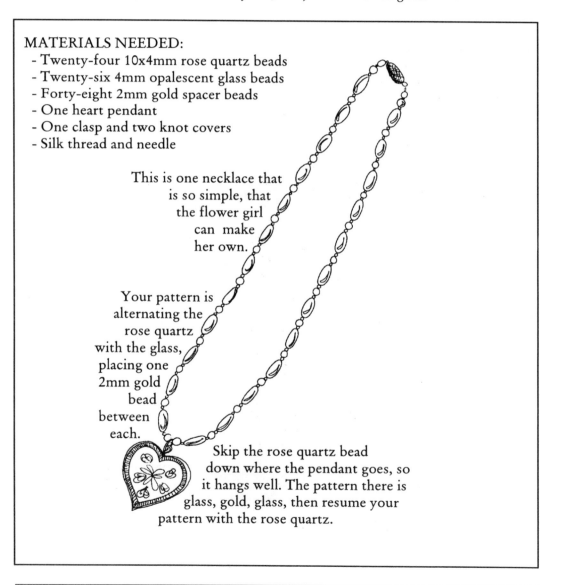

This is one necklace that is so simple, that the flower girl can make her own.

Your pattern is alternating the rose quartz with the glass, placing one 2mm gold bead between each.

Skip the rose quartz bead down where the pendant goes, so it hangs well. The pattern there is glass, gold, glass, then resume your pattern with the rose quartz.

# *Sweetheart Blue Topaz Necklace*

The faceted blue topaz and Czech lamp beads combine to make a beautiful look.

MATERIALS NEEDED:
- One 16" strand of faceted blue topaz beads
- Four 6mm white lamp beads
- Two 4mm white lamp beads
- One 8mm white lamp bead
- One head pin
- One sterling accent with three holes
- One clasp and four knot covers
- Silk thread and needle

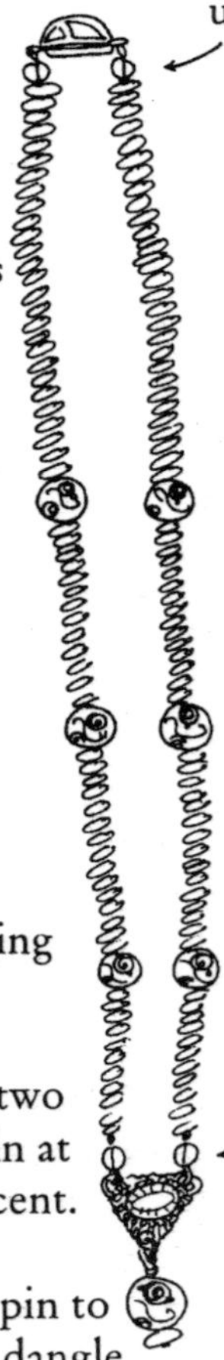

use a knot cover here
Use the basic stringing method.
It's like you're making two short necklaces that join at the clasp and the accent.
use a knot cover here
Use your head pin to make a dangle

# *Flower Girl Pearl Twist Necklace*

Using color-enhanced pearls in a multistrand necklace gives this necklace a charming look. Always make sure the color is stable and won't wear off.

MATERIALS NEEDED:
- Three 16" strands of freshwater pearls in pastel colors
- One heart locket and a large jumpring
- One clasp and two knot covers

You'll use the basic stringing method. The easy way to do this is to work one string at a time, and tape it to the table as you finish each strand.

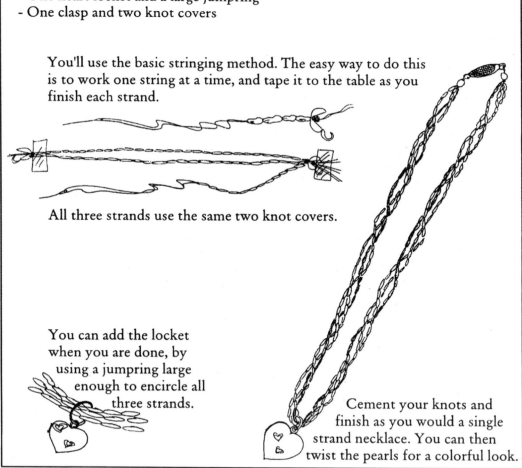

All three strands use the same two knot covers.

You can add the locket when you are done, by using a jumpring large enough to encircle all three strands.

Cement your knots and finish as you would a single strand necklace. You can then twist the pearls for a colorful look.

# Double Strand of Pearls

This is just like making two separate necklaces that are joined by a double clasp.

MATERIALS NEEDED:
- Two 16" strands of 6mm pearls
- One ornamental clasp
- Four knot covers

String each necklace
separately,
then
join.

If you use a pretty clasp, you can
wear it with the clasp in front.

You can make this necklace
any length, either
as a choker
or longer.

This type of choker is so elegant when you mix pearls and crystal together. Finding a beautiful clasp adds even more!

**MATERIALS NEEDED:**
- 126 5mm pearls
- Twenty four 5mm gyro cut (bicone) pink crystal
- Fifteen AB Green 6mm crystal
- Six pink rhinestone rondells
- Six AB clear crystals
- Four 3-hole separator bars
- Six knot covers and one elegant clasp with coordinating rhinestones
- Silk thread and a needle

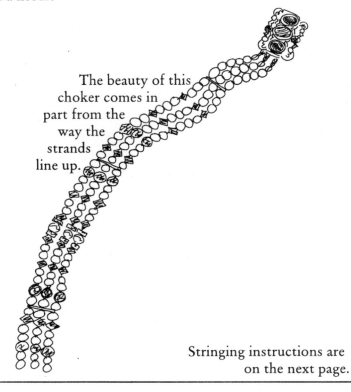

The beauty of this choker comes in part from the way the strands line up.

Stringing instructions are on the next page.

Work each strand individually. Use tape to hold the finished strands down as you work. <u>Don't</u> forget to include your separator bars!

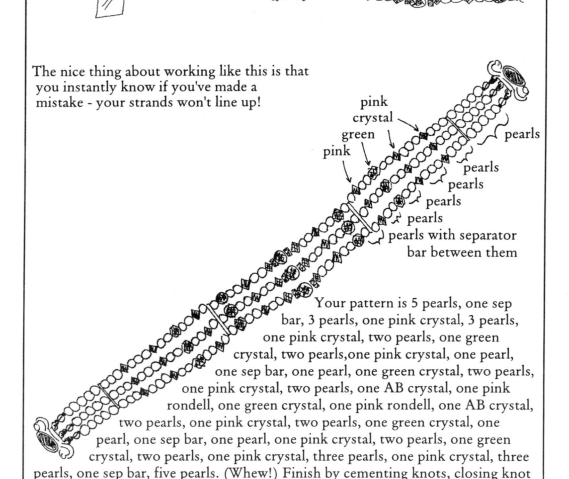

The nice thing about working like this is that you instantly know if you've made a mistake - your strands won't line up!

pink
crystal
green
pink

pearls

pearls
pearls
pearls
pearls
pearls with separator
bar between them

Your pattern is 5 pearls, one sep bar, 3 pearls, one pink crystal, 3 pearls, one pink crystal, two pearls, one green crystal, two pearls, one pink crystal, one pearl, one sep bar, one pearl, one green crystal, two pearls, one pink crystal, two pearls, one AB crystal, one pink rondell, one green crystal, one pink rondell, one AB crystal, two pearls, one pink crystal, two pearls, one green crystal, one pearl, one sep bar, one pearl, one pink crystal, two pearls, one green crystal, two pearls, one pink crystal, three pearls, one pink crystal, three pearls, one sep bar, five pearls. (Whew!) Finish by cementing knots, closing knot covers, and attaching to your clasp. Be careful not to twist the strands.

Sometimes you want to make a long necklace that doesn't need a clasp. That way, you can use a pearl shortener to create more than one look.

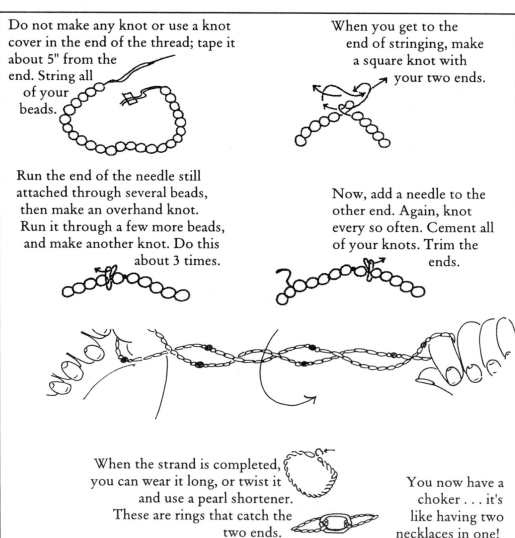

Do not make any knot or use a knot cover in the end of the thread; tape it about 5" from the end. String all of your beads.

When you get to the end of stringing, make a square knot with your two ends.

Run the end of the needle still attached through several beads, then make an overhand knot. Run it through a few more beads, and make another knot. Do this about 3 times.

Now, add a needle to the other end. Again, knot every so often. Cement all of your knots. Trim the ends.

When the strand is completed, you can wear it long, or twist it and use a pearl shortener. These are rings that catch the two ends.

You now have a choker . . . it's like having two necklaces in one!

There are several techniques of beading on fabric. These can be used for embellishing a wedding gown or bridesmaid's dress; to add a little something to a ring pillow; as a beaded accent on a lapel . . . almost anywhere. Use nymo thread and an English beading needle.

The THREE BEAD METHOD gives a lot of control about the placement of your beads. It's perfect for solid bead coverage.

Have a design in mind. Place your your fabric in an embroidery hoop. Make a knot on the wrong side, stitch thru to the right side.

After picking up 3 beads, stitch thru the fabric.

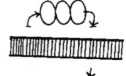

Bring up the needle just before the 3rd bead. Go thru that bead again, and and 3 more beads. Repeat until you're done.

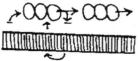

You can also work this with 4 or 5 beads at a time, too.

The SATIN STITCH is very quick. Many bridal gowns are already beaded with this stitch.

String 2" of beads on your thread.

Pass the needle thru the cloth. Repeat again, parallel to the first row.

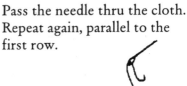

You can leave these stitches loose, or go back and tack them down.

COUCHING can be done with one needle or two.

With the ONE needle method, after you sew your beads on in rows, you circle back and tack down your stitches.

With the two needle method, the first needle strings the beads onto one long strand.

The second needle follows, and catches the first thread to tack it down at intervals.

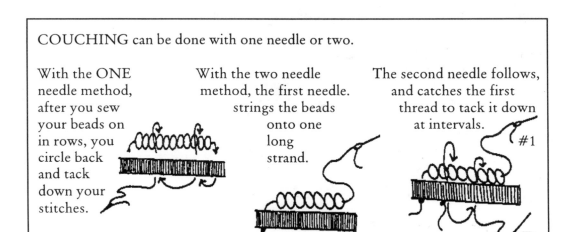

#1

#2

The CONTINENTAL STITCH is used for needlepoint, but this time we're adding a bead as we stitch. This is a great way to dress up netting. You can bead your veil with this technique.

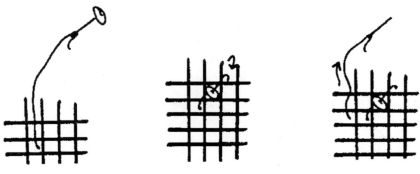

Try experimenting with different stitches and beads. You can make an inexpensive gown look like a designer creation with just a little practice.

# Simple Beaded Headpiece

This is a simple yet elegant hair ornament you can make quite easily. You can use ribbon, or beads-by-the-foot (available in most craft stores). You use those plastic combs that were so popular a few years back, and 24 gauge wire.

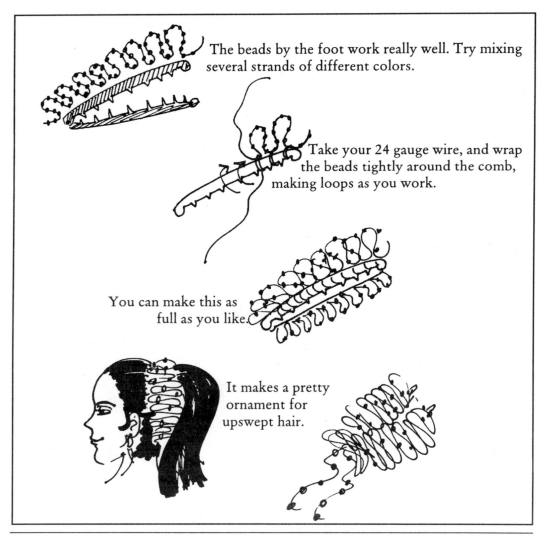

The beads by the foot work really well. Try mixing several strands of different colors.

Take your 24 gauge wire, and wrap the beads tightly around the comb, making loops as you work.

You can make this as full as you like.

It makes a pretty ornament for upswept hair.

# Classic Headpiece

This heirloom quality headpiece is very easy to make, using the techniques from the section on Beading on Fabric. You can make this in about 3 hours. This would cost you about $220 in the bridal stores.

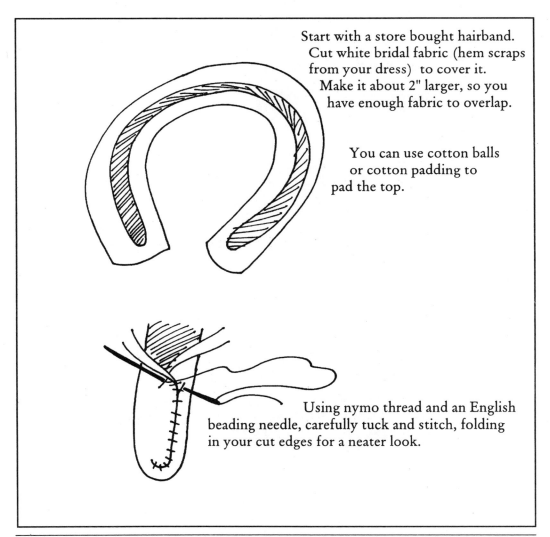

Start with a store bought hairband. Cut white bridal fabric (hem scraps from your dress) to cover it. Make it about 2" larger, so you have enough fabric to overlap.

You can use cotton balls or cotton padding to pad the top.

Using nymo thread and an English beading needle, carefully tuck and stitch, folding in your cut edges for a neater look.

Using the Satin stitch, start beading around the top of the hairband. You can use a pattern (I alternated rows of crystal, blue oval plastic pearls, and round 4mm plastic pearls. It took less than one 60" strand of each). If you want your fabric to show, stitch your rows further apart. If you want to cover it completely, then stitch closer.

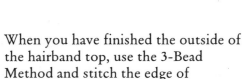

When you have finished the outside of the hairband top, use the 3-Bead Method and stitch the edge of the band with the 4mm pearls.

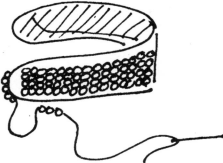

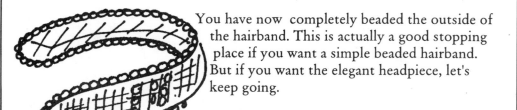

You have now completely beaded the outside of the hairband. This is actually a good stopping place if you want a simple beaded hairband. But if you want the elegant headpiece, let's keep going.

*The Beaded Jewelry For A Wedding Book*

Create fringe by adding beads and crystals to the ends of the hairband. Go down through the beads, put one small one on to act as a "pivot bead", then back up through all the others. Don't go back through the pivot bead, because then all of your beads will fall off.
Make a couple of stitches in the band to secure, then on to the next fringe.

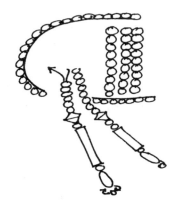

When you're done, sew or glue small satin roses to cover the stitches of your fringe, or you can cover with loops of beadwork.

This headpiece is worn like a crown, and the fringe hangs beautifully at the sides.

## VARIATION:

You can buy netting starting at about $2 per yard.

Using a large basting stitch on your sewing machine, you can pull the threads to gather them into pleats.

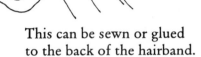

This can be sewn or glued to the back of the hairband.

## OTHER VARIATIONS:

- Take a pretty piece of ribbon and make a "halo" type headpiece. You can then embellish it with beads.

- To make a pretty "mantilla" effect, take lace veiling and bead it. You can use sequins, beads, and ribbons.

- Experiment with fabric-covering combs, hairbands, and other everyday hair ornaments, then bead them with fringe, rhinestones by the foot, etc.

# *About the Author*

Wendy Simpson Conner is no stranger to beads. As a third-generation bead artist, she grew up with beads from a very early age. Her grandmother was the jewelry and costume designer for the Ziegfeld Follies.

Being from a creative family, Wendy spent her childhood doing many types of crafts in a rural community. ("There just wasn 't anything else to do!"). Over the years, she has mastered many techniques, but beads remained her first love.

She worked as a designer in television for awhile, and also has a strong illustration background (she always insists on doing her own illustrations).

Wendy has been teaching vocational beadwork classes for San Diego Community Colleges and the Grossmont Adult School District for fifteen years. She not only teaches beading technique, but also the dynamics of running your own jewelry business.

Wendy designs jewelry for several television shows, as well as the celebrities on them.

She is currently involved with a documentary being made about beads.

Her first book, *The Best Little Beading Book,* was the result of many of her classroom handouts. All of her books, including *The Beaded Lampshade Book, The Magical Beaded Medicine Bag Book, The "Knotty" Macrame and Beading Book, The Beaded Watchband Book* and *The Chain & Crystal Book,* have been very popular. They are part of **The Beading Books Series,** a collection of 25 books devoted to preserving beading techniques and history.

Wendy is available to teach workshops. If you are interested, please contact her through the Interstellar Publishing Company, Post Office Box 2215, La Mesa, California, 91943.

# INTERSTELLAR
## TRADING & PUBLISHING COMPANY

**Other Books By the
Interstellar Trading & Publishing Company:**

If you would like a list of other titles and forthcoming books from the Interstellar Trading & Publishing Company, please send a stamped, self-addressed envelope to:

**THE INTERSTELLAR TRADING & PUBLISHING COMPANY
POST OFFICE BOX 2215
LA MESA, CALIFORNIA, 91943**